PIANO · VOCAL · GUITAR

CHRIS STAPLETON
TRAVELLER

ISBN 978-1-4950-6512-5

7777 W. BLUEMOUND RD. P.O. BOX 13819 MILWAUKEE, WI 53213

Visit Hal Leonard Online at
www.halleonard.com

TRAVELLER

Words and Music by
CHRIS STAPLETON

FIRE AWAY

Words and Music by CHRIS STAPLETON
and THOMAS DANIEL GREEN

TENNESSEE WHISKEY

Words and Music by DEAN DILLON
and LINDA HARGROVE

as a glass _ of bran - dy, and, hon - ey, I ___ stay

stoned ___ on your love ___ all ___ the time. ___

PARACHUTE

Words and Music by CHRIS STAPLETON
and JIM BEAVERS

Moderately

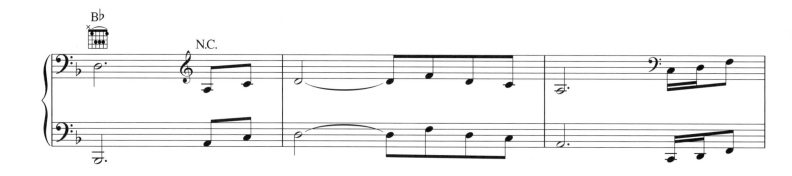

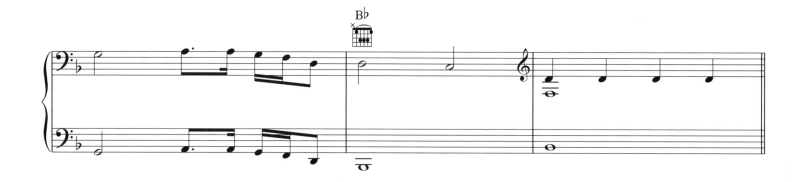

Street lights a - long___ the high - way
There's a song that I___ re - mem - ber,

* *Recorded a half step higher.*

If you think you're go - in' down,

just know I will be a - round.

D.S. al Coda

You ___

CODA

___ ba - by, I ___ will be your ___

WHISKEY AND YOU

Words and Music by CHRIS STAPLETON
and LEE THOMAS MILLER

There's ___ a bot - tle
I've ___ got a prob - lem, row

on the dress - er by ___ your ___ ring. ___ And it's emp -
I can walk ___ in an - y ___ store. ___ It ain't a
but it ain't ___ like what ___ you ___ think. ___ I

NOBODY TO BLAME

Words and Music by CHRIS STAPLETON,
RONNIE BOWMAN and BARRY BALES

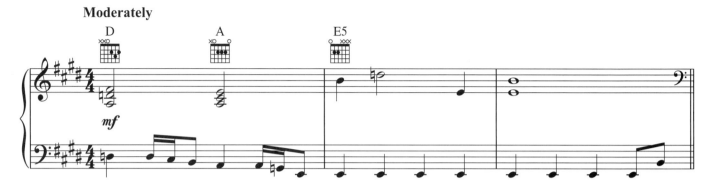

She took down the pho-to-graph of our wed-ding day,
fired up my old hot-rod, ran it in the pond, put

ripped it down the mid-dle and threw my half a-way. And I got
sug-ar in my John Deere; I can't e-ven mow my lawn. And I got

MORE OF YOU

Words and Music by CHRIS STAPLETON
and RONNIE BOWMAN

it makes me want

more of you.

WHEN THE STARS COME OUT

Words and Music by CHRIS STAPLETON
and DAN WILSON

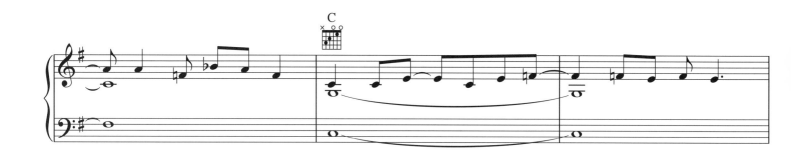

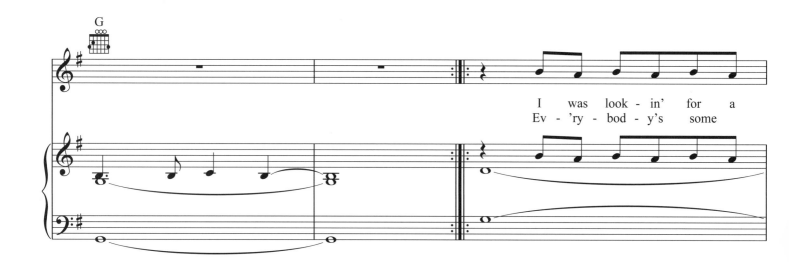

I was look-in' for a
Ev-'ry-bod-y's some

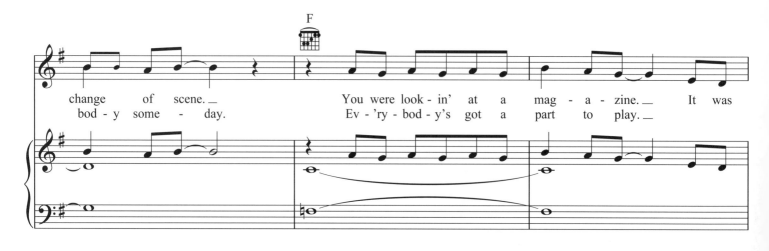

change of scene.___ You were look-in' at a mag-a-zine.___ It was
bod-y some-day. Ev-'ry-bod-y's got a part to play.___

D.S. al Coda

DADDY DOESN'T PRAY ANYMORE

Words and Music by
CHRIS STAPLETON

Dad - dy _____ does - n't pray _____ an - y - more.

There was a

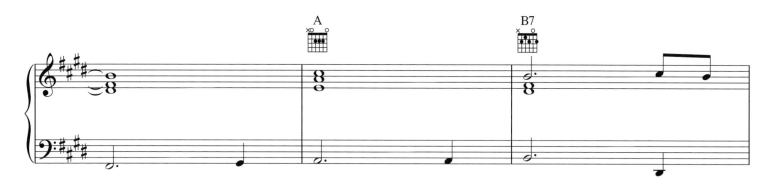

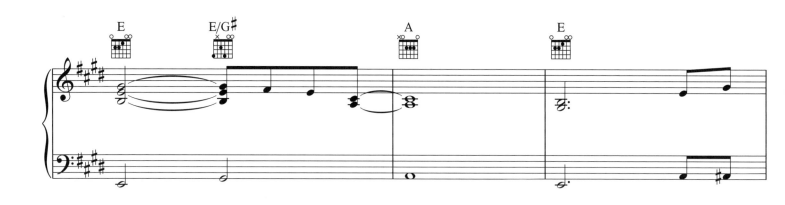

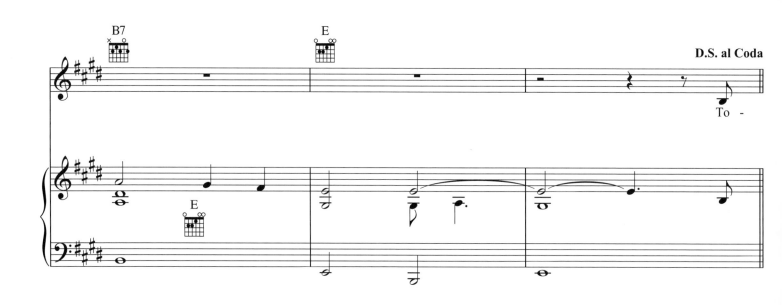

MIGHT AS WELL GET STONED

Words and Music by CHRIS STAPLETON
and JIMMY STEWART

Ev-'ry time I watch the

WAS IT 26

Words and Music by
DON SAMPSON

64

Now

THE DEVIL NAMED MUSIC

Words and Music by
CHRIS STAPLETON

dev - il named mu - sic____ is tak - in' my____ life.

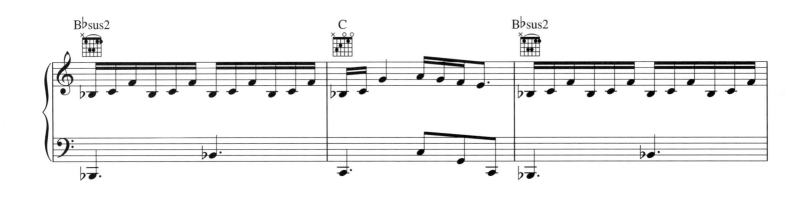

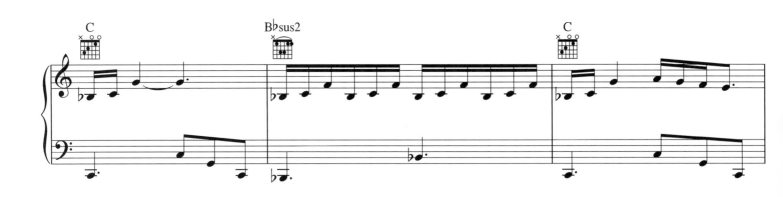

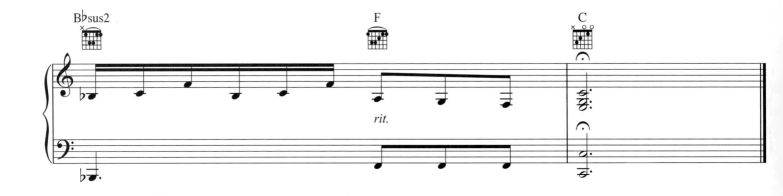

OUTLAW STATE OF MIND

Words and Music by CHRIS STAPLETON,
RONNIE BOWMAN and JERRY SALLEY

Moderately

out - law ___ state of mind. ___

rit.　*a tempo*

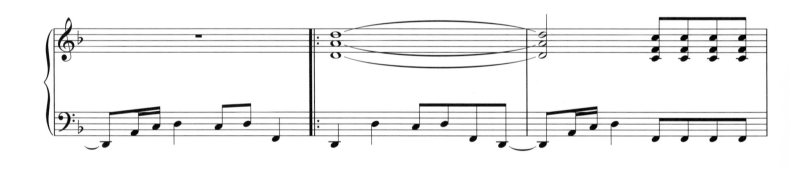

Repeat ad lib.

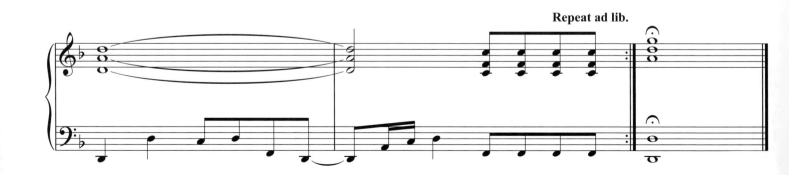

SOMETIMES I CRY

Words and Music by CHRIS STAPLETON
and CLINT INGERSOLL